Penguins

Penguins

Jenny Markert

THE CHILD'S WORLD®, INC.

Library of Congress Cataloging-in-Publication Data
Markert, Jenny.
Penguins / by Jenny Markert.
p.   cm.
Includes index.
Summary: Describes the physical characteristics,
behavior, habitat, and life cycle of penguins.
ISBN 1-56766-490-3 (lib. bdg. : alk paper)
1. Penguins—Juvenile literature.   [1. Penguins.]   I. Title.
QL696.S473M35   1998
598.47—dc21   97-27836
CIP
AC

Photo Credits

© Art Wolfe/Tony Stone Images: 6
© Daniel J. Cox/Natural Exposures: 16, 23, 30
© John G. Shedd Aquarium: 15
© Kevin Schafer/Tony Stone Images: 13
© 1995 Mark J. Thomas/Dembinsky Photo Assoc. Inc: 24, 26
© 1997 Rod Planck/Dembinsky Photo Assoc. Inc: cover, 2, 9, 10
© Kevin Schafer: 20
© Tony Stone Images: 29

On the cover...

Front cover: *King penguins* like this one are very beautiful.
Page 2: This *macaroni penguin* is standing on a rock.

Table of Contents

Far away in a frozen land, snowy winds howl. Icebergs float quietly. Freezing waters slosh on the shore. Suddenly, an animal shoots out of the cold water and lands on the ice. It shakes the water off its body and waddles away happily. What could this strange animal be? It's a penguin!

⇐ This *Adélie penguin* is standing on an icy shore.

What Do Penguins Look Like?

Penguins are birds, but they cannot fly. Instead, they spend most of their lives in the ocean. They have smooth, sleek bodies that are perfect for swimming. Penguins have powerful **flippers** instead of wings. They use their flippers to move quickly through the water. Penguins can swim faster than most people can run.

Penguins have white bellies and dark backs. They look as though they are wearing little suits! Their coloring protects them from their enemies. When they swim, penguins are hard to see.

This *gentoo penguin* has just finished swimming. ⇒

There are 18 different kinds of penguins. Each kind looks different. *Emperor penguins* are four feet tall and weigh over 100 pounds. *Rockhopper penguins* are smaller penguins with red eyes and white feet. *Macaroni penguins* have yellow feathers on their eyebrows. *Adélie* (uh–DAY–lee) *penguins* have white eyelids and a red beak.

Where Do Penguins Live?

Penguins live only in the southern parts of the world. Many live in areas that have very cold weather. Some penguins even live on the thick ice around the continent of Antarctica. Antarctica is the coldest place on Earth. In the winter, the temperature can drop to 100 degrees below zero! Antarctica is covered with snow and ice, even during the summer.

These *emperor penguins* live in Antarctica. ⇒

How Do Penguins Stay Warm?

Penguins are perfectly made for living in the cold. They have a warm coat of feathers. A penguin's outer feathers are small and packed tightly together. They are covered with a special oil the penguin makes inside its body. The oil makes the penguins waterproof.

Beneath these outer feathers, penguins have a layer of warm, fluffy feathers called **down**. Under their skin, penguins also have a thick layer of fat. The fat keeps the penguins extra warm. But sometimes, penguins get too hot. When this happens, they simply fluff up their feathers so the warm air can escape.

It is easy to see how closely packed a penguin's feathers are. ⇒

Penguins spend much of their time swimming in the cold, icy water. They can dive far beneath the surface. Many penguins can hold their breath for almost 20 minutes!

Penguins find their food in the ocean. They eat fish and tiny animals called *krill*. They also like to eat squid and crabs. A penguin's mouth is filled with rough spines. These spines help the penguin hold onto slippery fish or squid that might try to get away.

Do Penguins Have Any Enemies?

Krill and fish are not the only things that swim in the ocean. Many **predators** live there, too. Predators are animals that hunt other animals for food. Sharks and killer whales are predators that like to eat penguins. But the penguin's worst enemy is the *leopard seal*. Leopard seals are fast swimmers and can catch any penguin that isn't careful.

Leopard seals like this one have very sharp teeth. ⇒

The only way a penguin can escape a hungry predator is to get out of the water. But many cold areas have slippery ice all along the edge of the ocean. To get onto the ice, the penguins swim down very deep. Then they paddle straight toward the surface. They shoot out of the water and onto the ice!

← These emperor penguins are quickly getting out of the water.

How Do Penguins Move Around?

When they are out of the water, penguins stand on their fat little legs. They waddle when they walk because their legs are so short. When they get tired of waddling, some penguins plop down on their bellies. If the ground is icy, the penguins can slide on their bellies. Sliding is much faster than walking—and probably a lot more fun!

These emperor penguins have found an easy way to get around. ⇒

How Do Penguins Have Babies?

When the time is right, penguins gather into huge nesting areas called **rookeries**. Some rookeries are far out on the snowy ice. Others are on rocky cliffs.

In the rookery, each female penguin lays one or two eggs. Some penguins make nests for their eggs out of stones or grass. In colder areas, penguins do not build nests. Instead, they balance their eggs on their feet! A thick fold of skin covers the egg and keeps it warm and safe.

What Are Baby Penguins Like?

After a short time, the baby penguins break out of their shells. These baby penguins are called **chicks**. The chicks are covered with soft, fluffy down. Chicks often hide in their parents' feathers to keep warm. The chicks eat food that is stored in their parents' throats. To find the food, the baby penguins stick their heads deep into their parents' mouths.

← This emperor penguin is caring for its chick.

The little penguins grow very fast. Soon they lose their fluffy down and grow their adult feathers. They also learn how to waddle around. When the chicks are a little older, their parents bring them to the seashore. Instead of being afraid, the young penguins jump right into the water. They do not even need swimming lessons!

These Adélie penguins are all going for a swim. ⇒

Penguins are wonderful animals that are perfectly made for living in the cold. The land where they live looks lonely, but the penguins are right at home. So the next time you shiver on a cold winter day, think about the penguin. Maybe you can learn to like the cold, too!

Glossary

chicks (CHIKS)
Many baby birds are called chicks. Penguin chicks keep warm by hiding in their parents' feathers.

down (DOWN)
Down is a layer of warm, fluffy feathers next to a penguin's skin. The down keeps the penguin warm.

flippers (FLIH–perz)
Instead of wings, penguins have flippers. These powerful flippers help the penguin move quickly through the water.

predators (PREH–duh–terz)
Predators are animals that hunt other animals for food. Sharks, killer whales, and leopards seals are predators that like to eat penguins.

rookeries (RU–kuh–reez)
Rookeries are large nesting areas. Penguins gather in rookeries to raise their babies.

Index